I Can

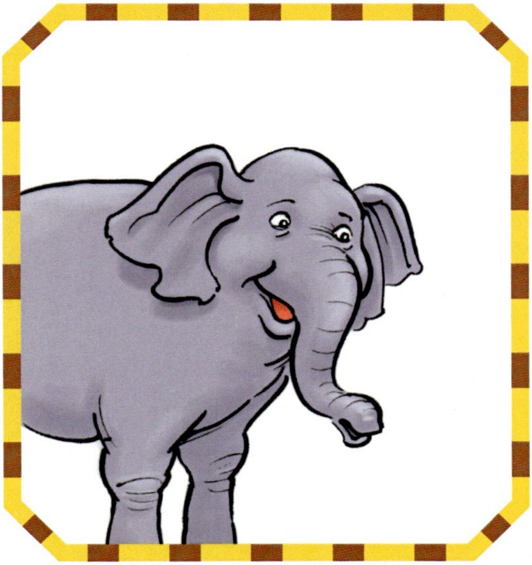

Illustrated by Paul Könye

PEARSON

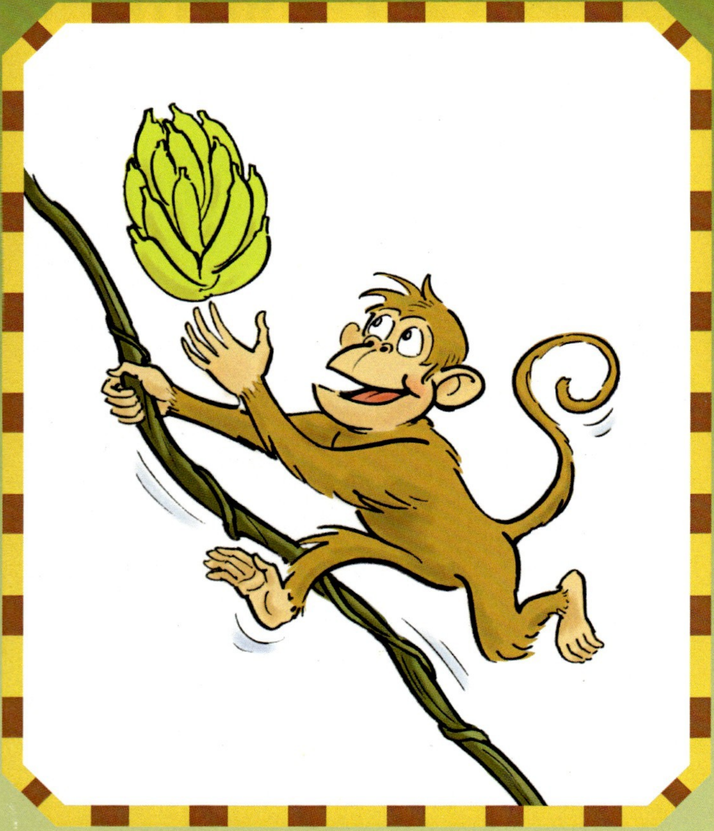

I can swing.

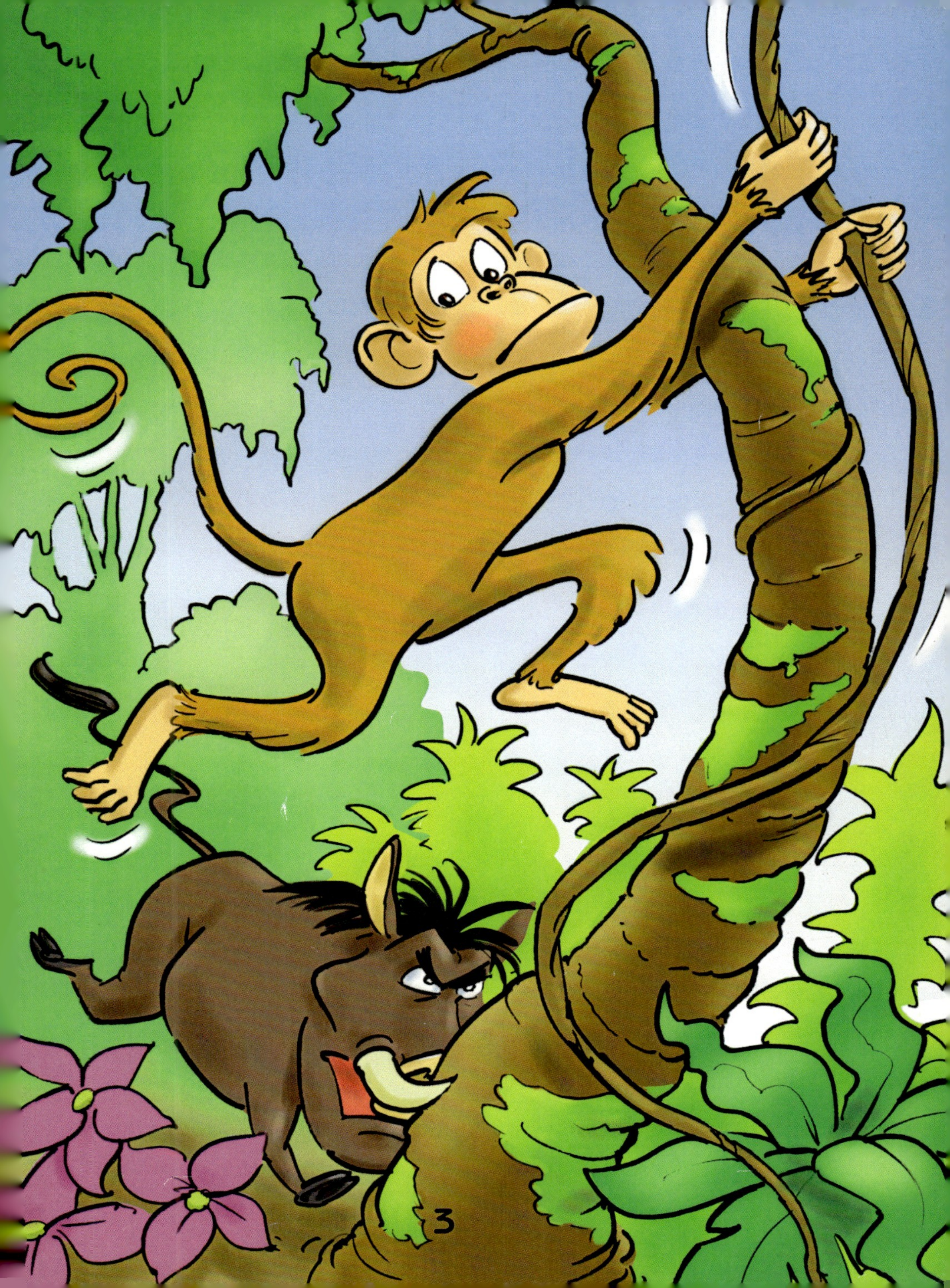

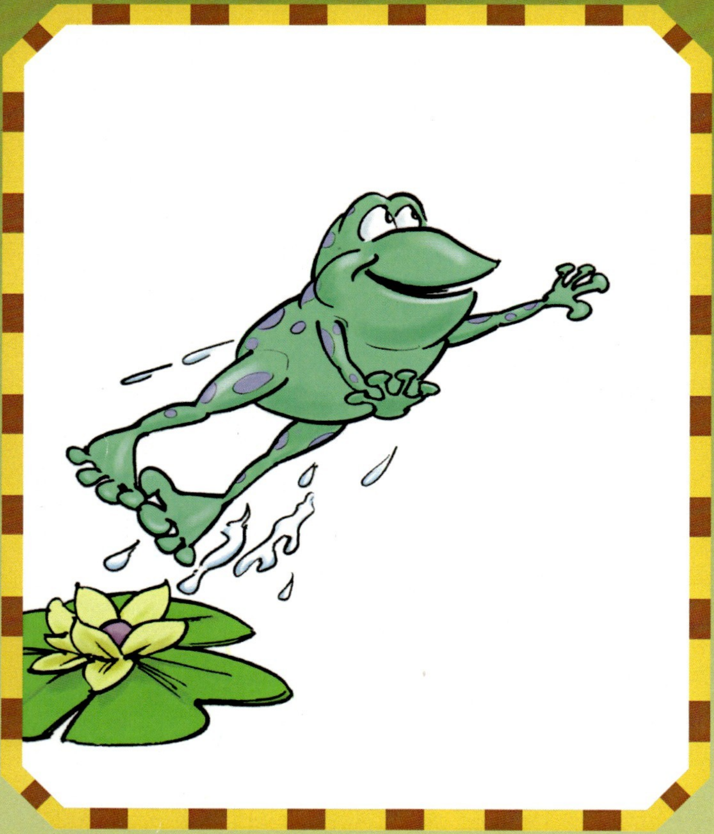

I can jump.

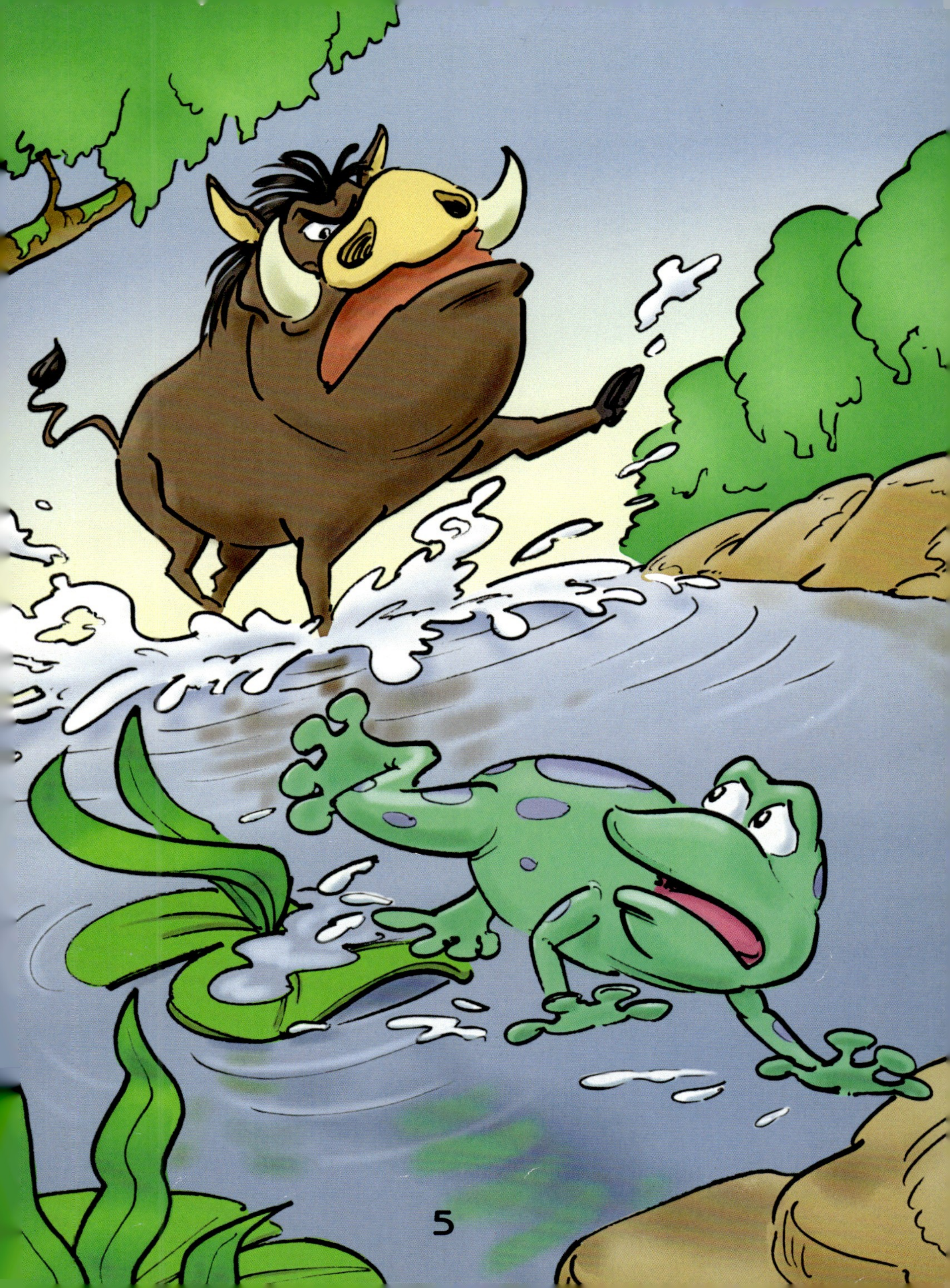

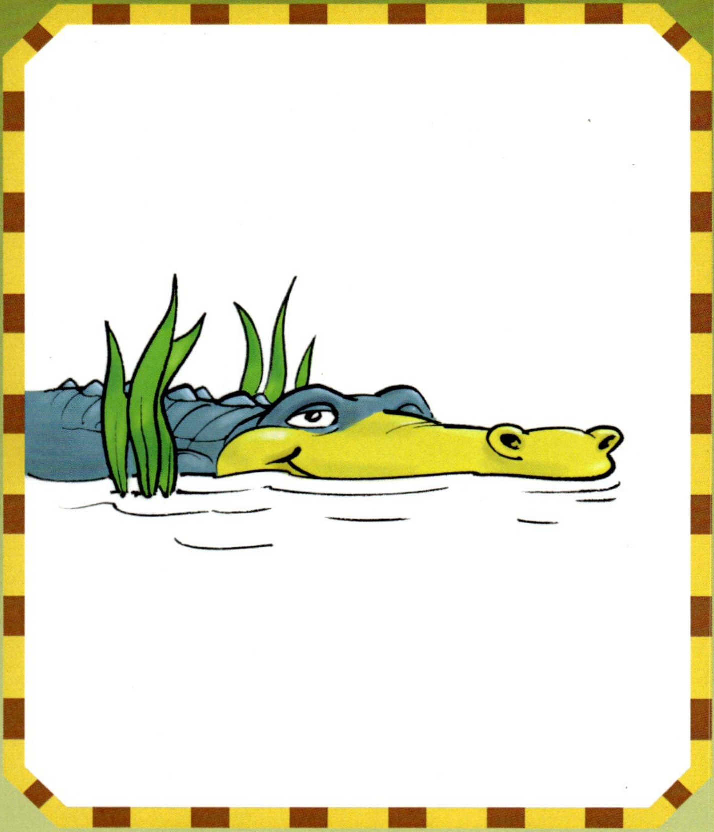

I can swim.

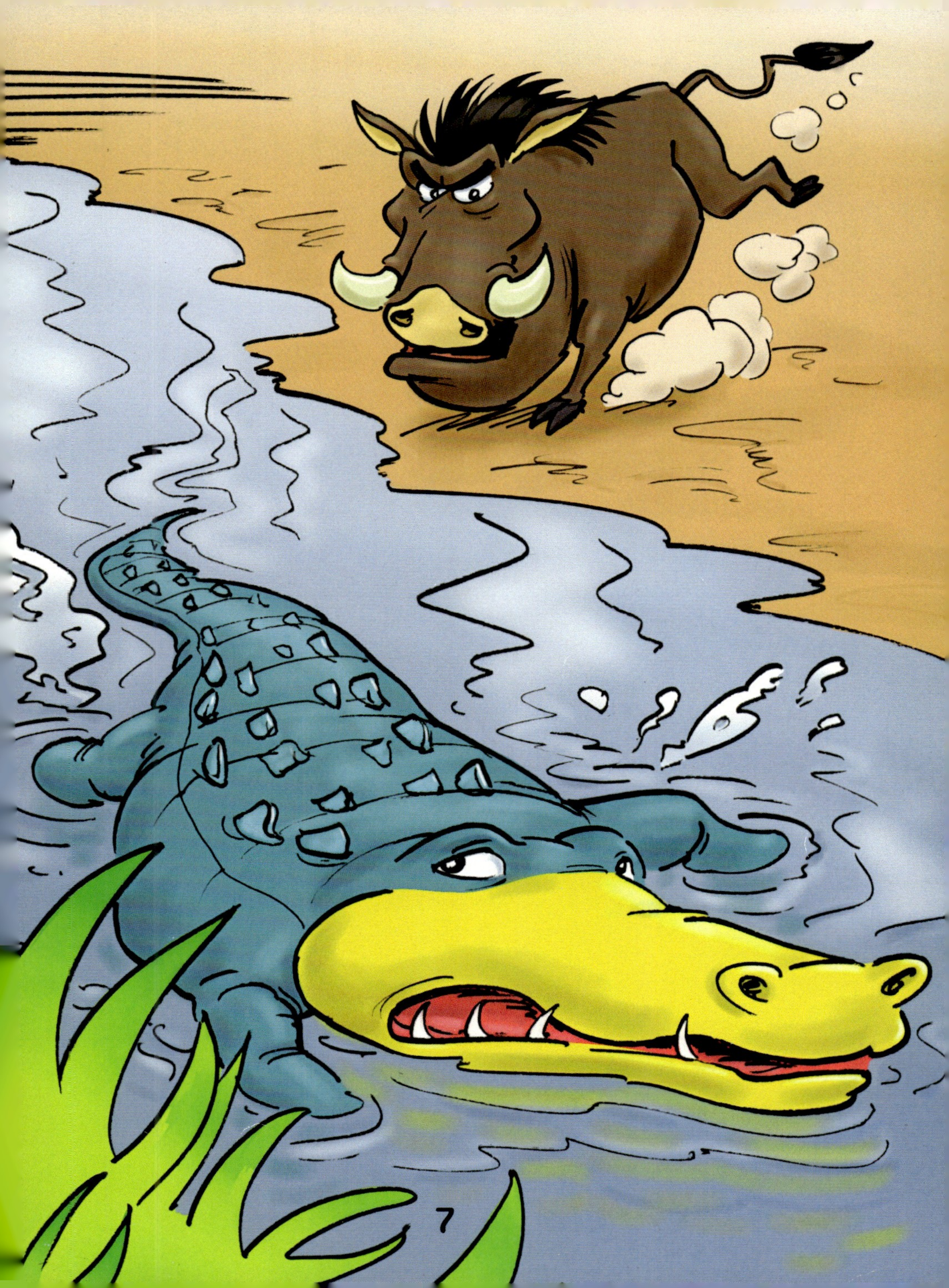

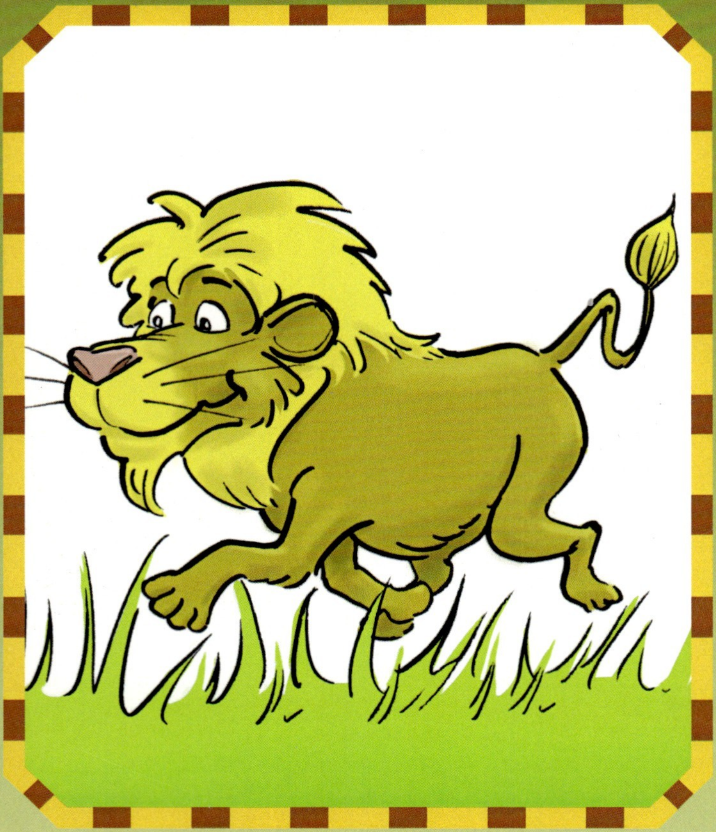

I can run.

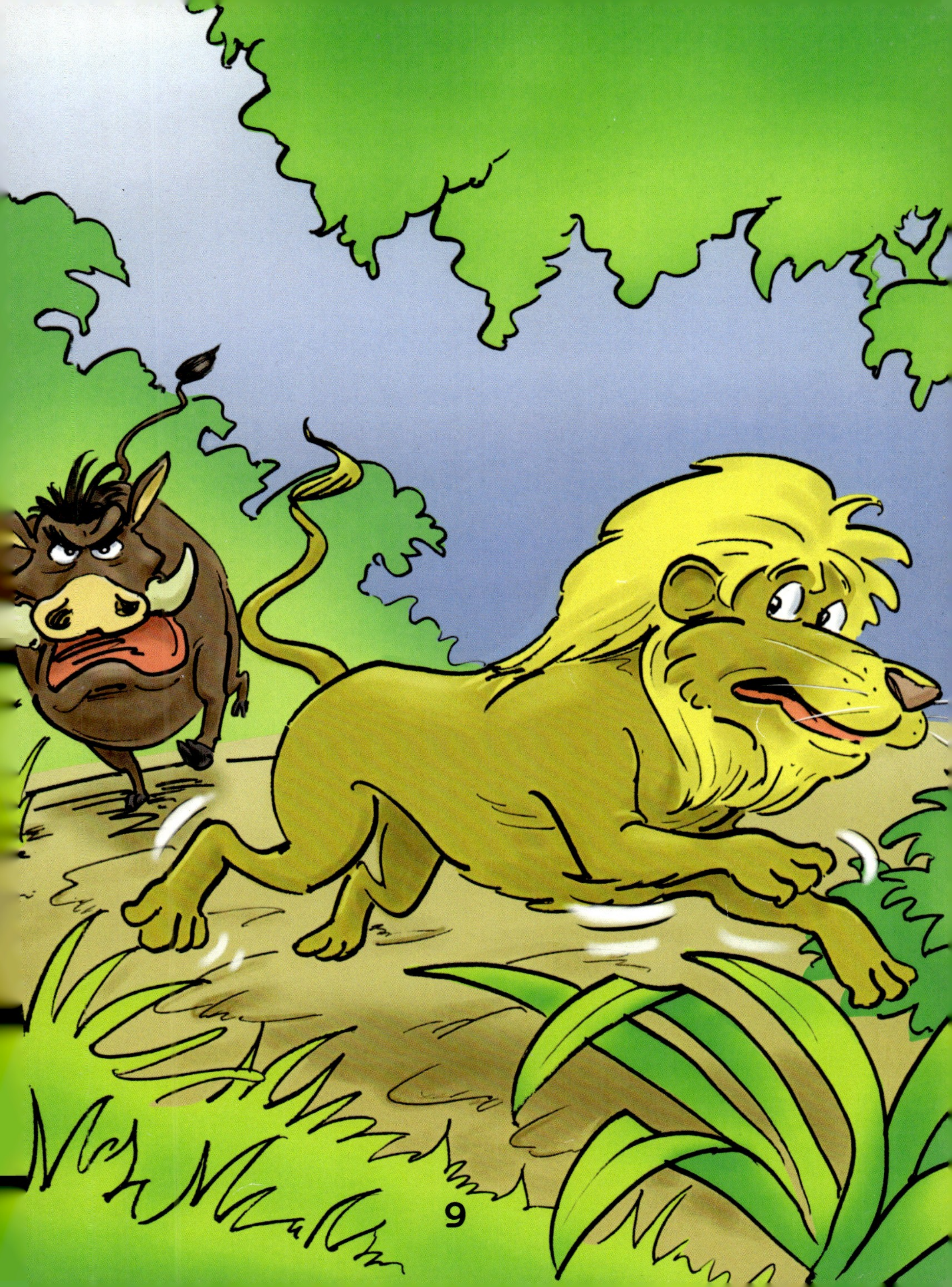

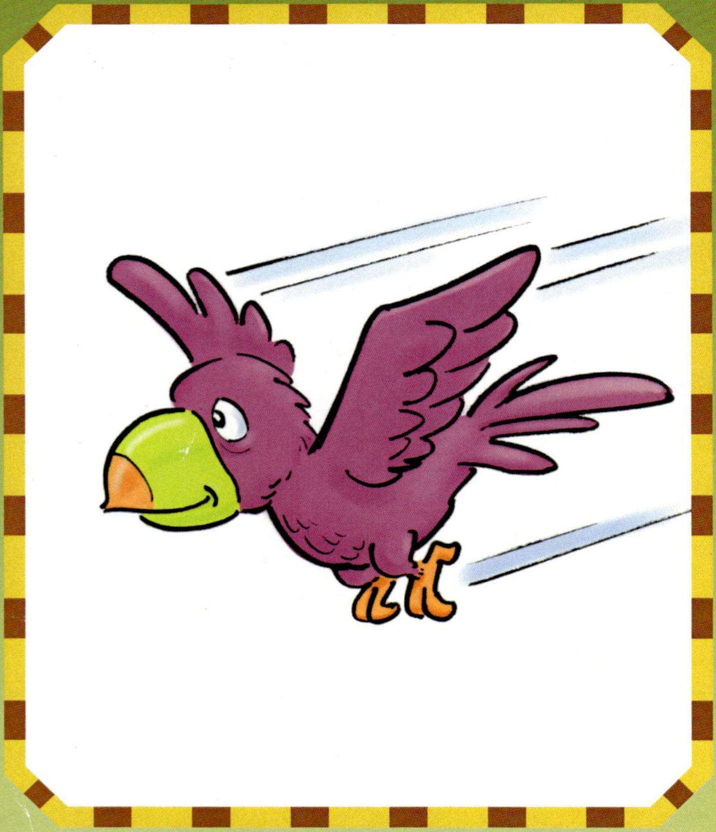

I can fly.

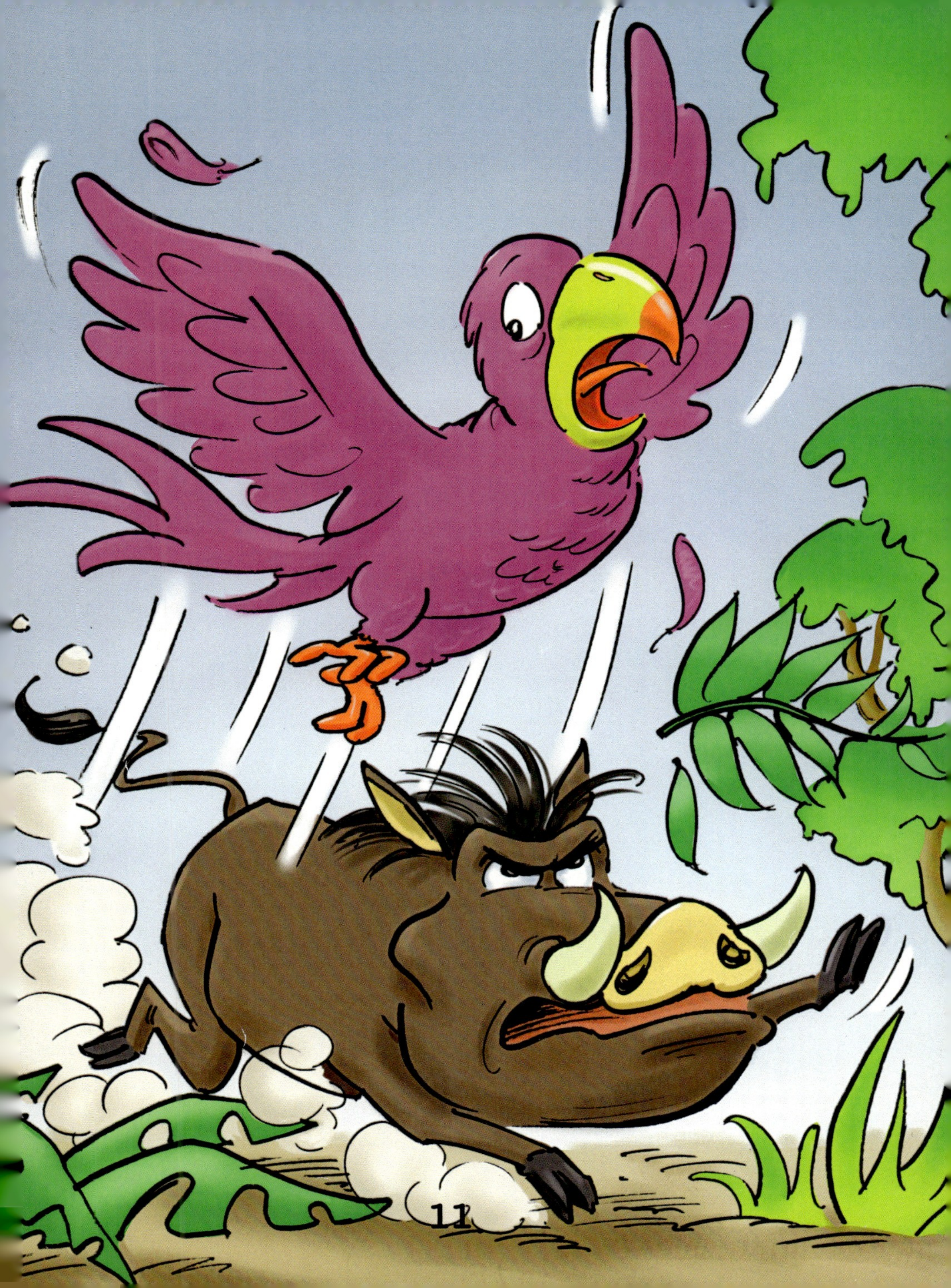

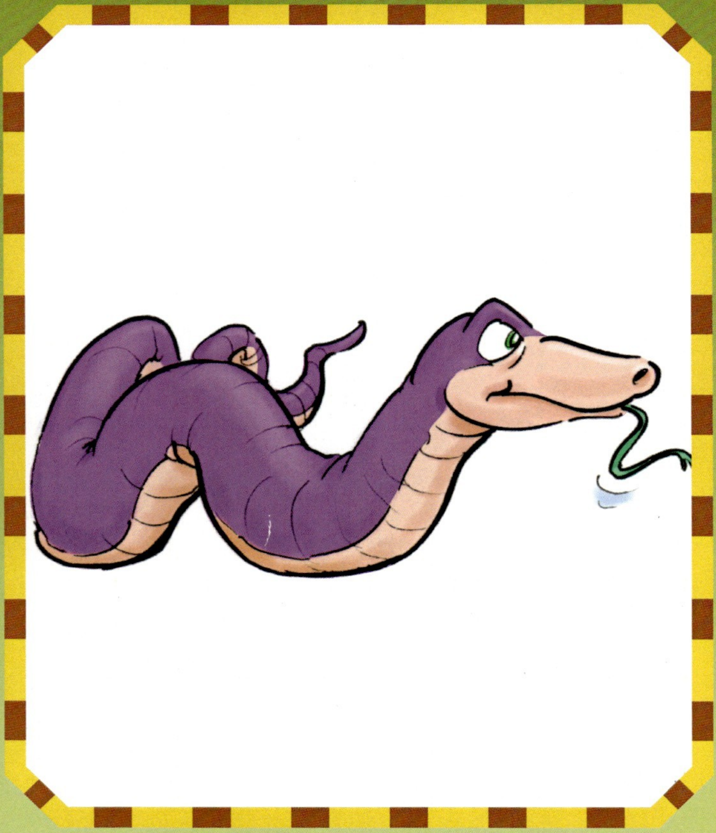

I can slide.

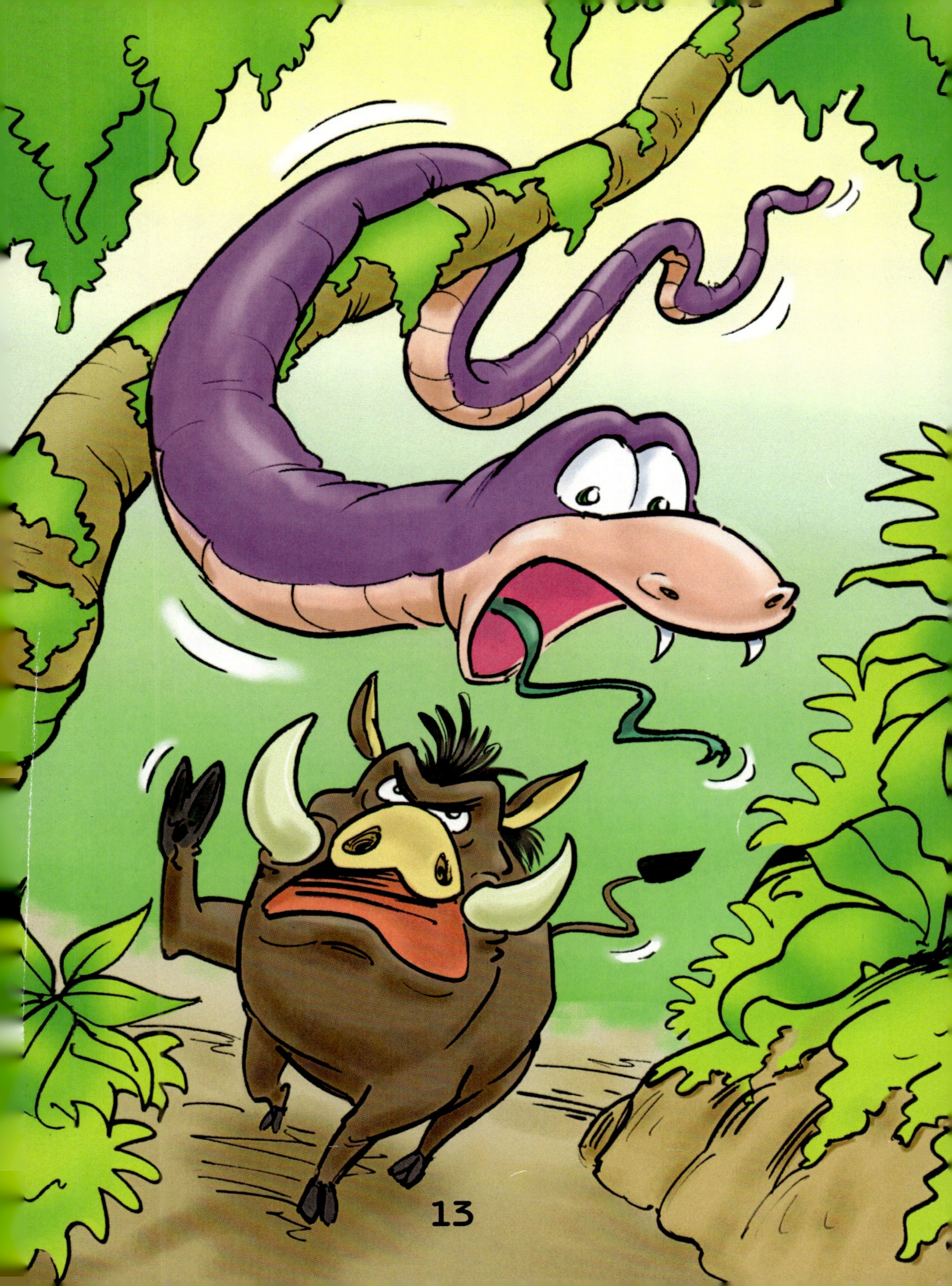

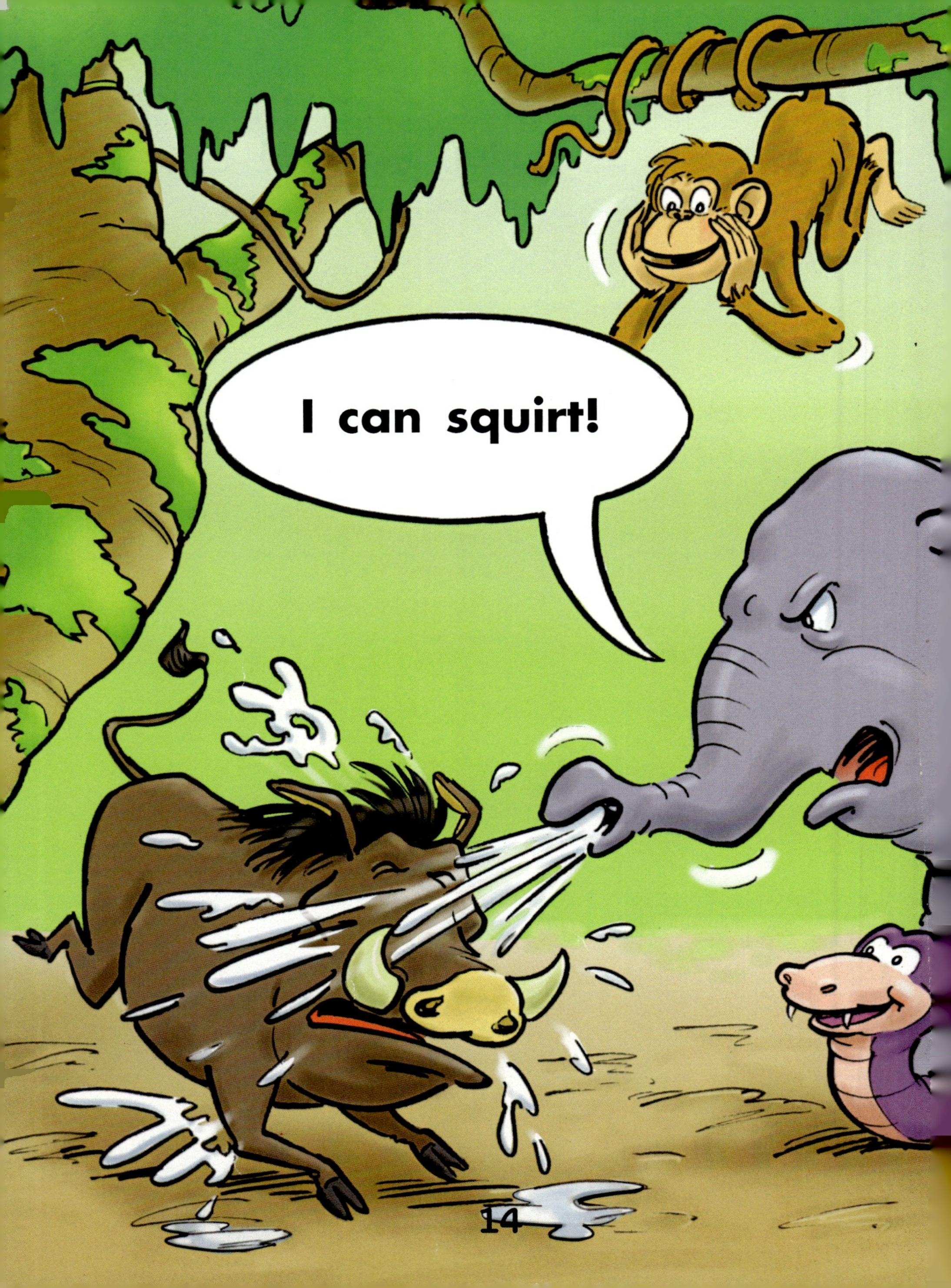
I can squirt!

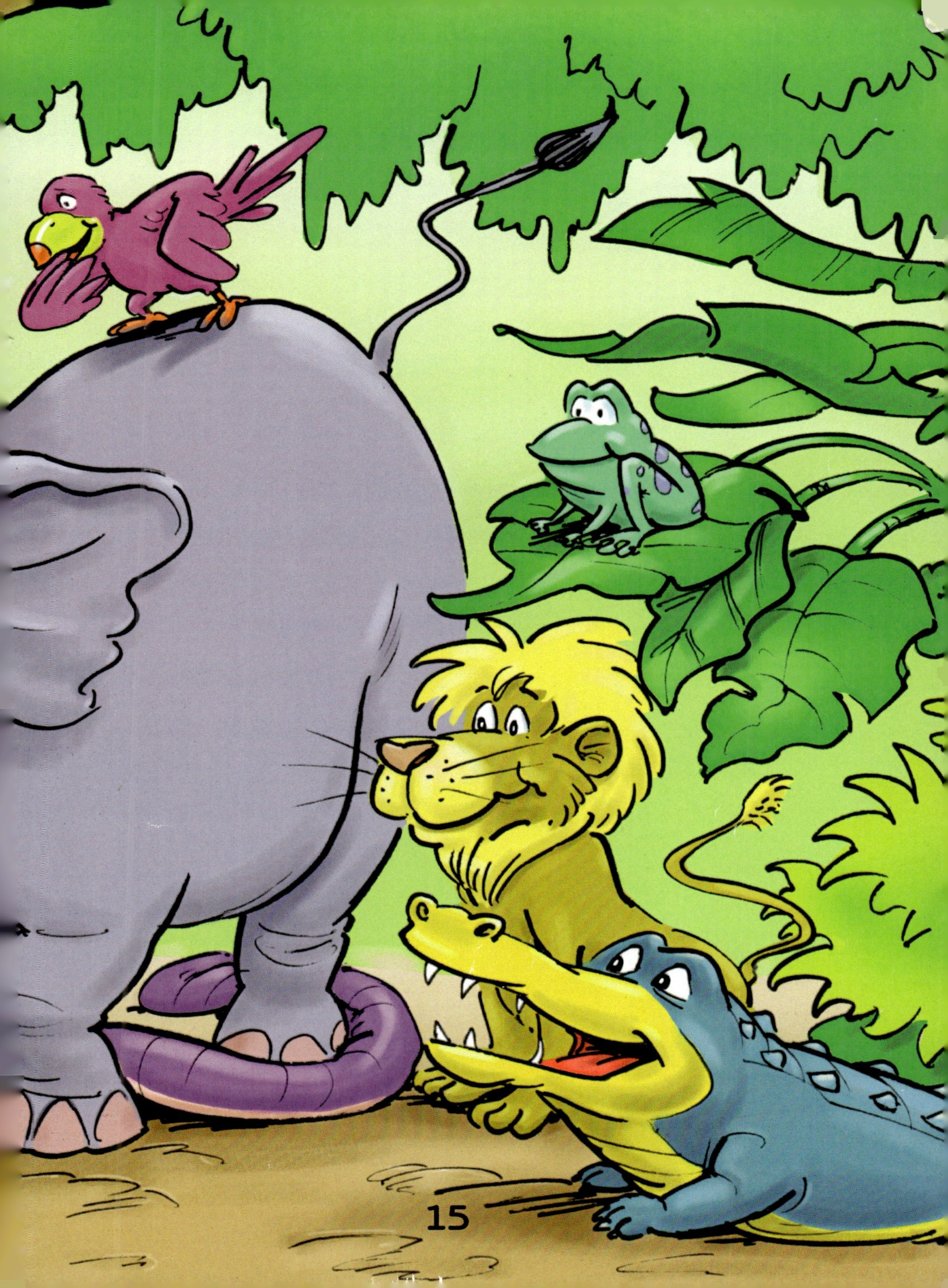

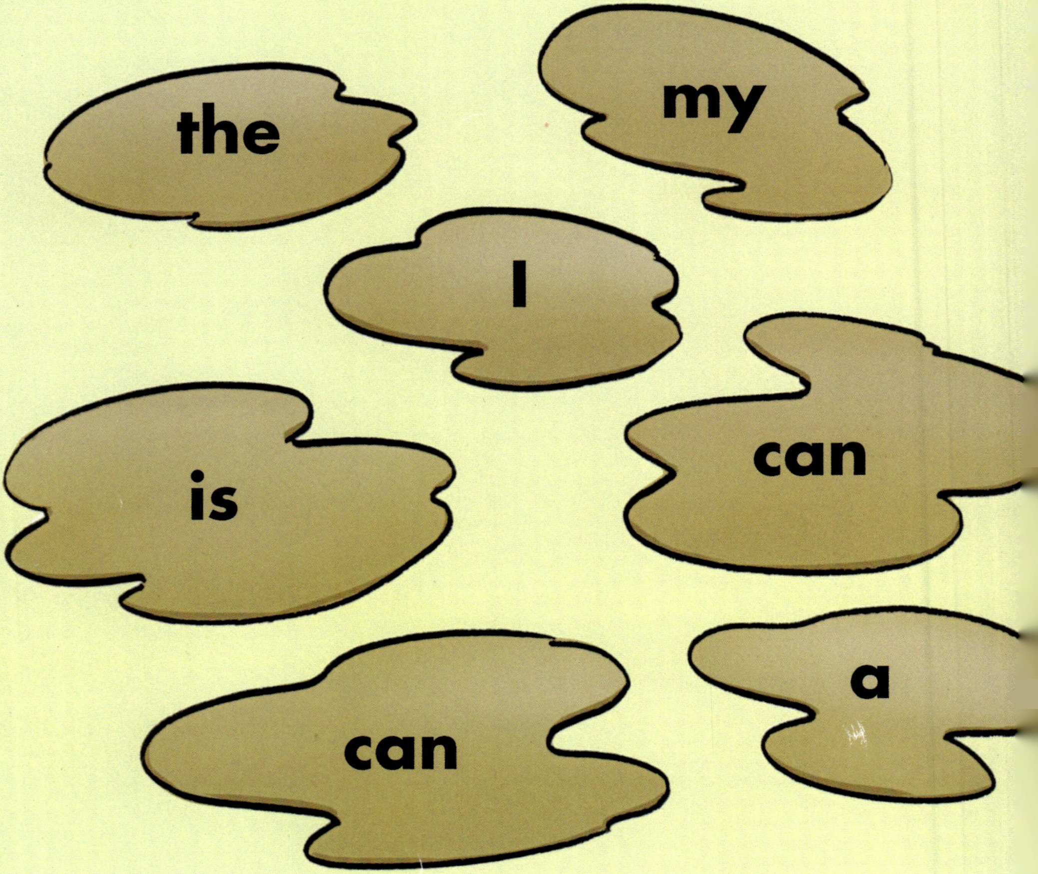
the
my
I
is
can
can
a